NORTH NORFOLK RAILWAY ALBUM

BRIAN FISHER

BECKNELL BOOKS
NORWICH AND KING'S LYNN

First published 1981

ISBN 0 907087 05 1

BECKNELL BOOKS
P.O. BOX 21
KING'S LYNN
PE30 2QP

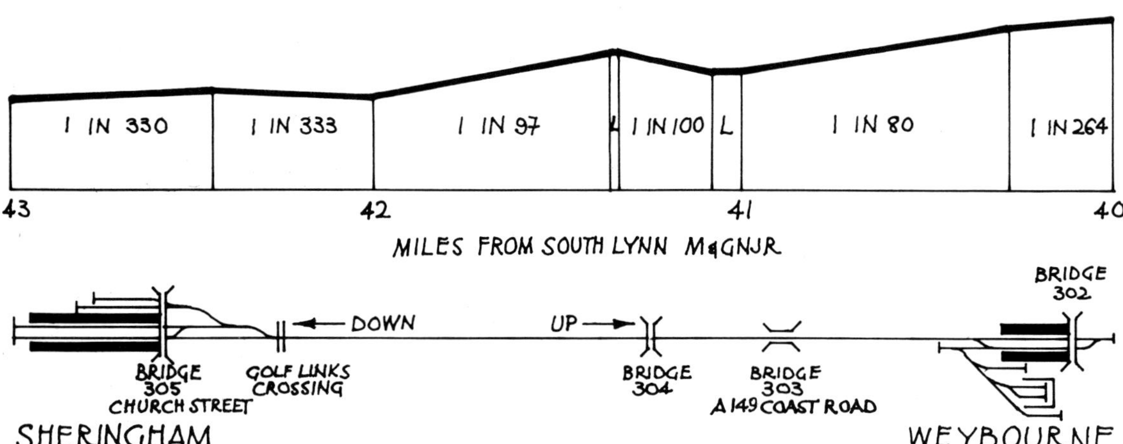

SECTION OPENED BY EASTERN & MIDLANDS RAILWAY 16TH JUNE 1887. M&GNJR FORMED 1ST JULY 1893. WEYBOURNE STATION OPENED 1ST JULY 1901. LNER TAKEOVER 1ST OCTOBER 1936. NATIONALISED 1ST JAN 1948 CLOSED TO TRAFFIC 6TH APRIL 1964. M&GNJRS STOCK DELIVERY 14TH JUNE 1967. LIGHT RAILWAY ORDER 6TH APRIL 1976

NORTH NORFOLK RAILWAY

Designed by Becknell Studio

Printed in Great Britain by Witley Press Ltd., Hunstanton

Introduction

The problem with compiling an album of photographs of the North Norfolk Railway is really one of what to leave out rather than what to put in! So much has happened since those tentative meetings of the Midland and Great Northern Joint Railway Preservation Society — as it was then — shortly after the closure of most of the old M&GN system in February 1959. The Society, one of the pioneers of the standard-gauge preservation movement, had the vision and determination to raise the money to buy examples of two widely-used classes of typical East Anglian steam locomotives — the J15 and B12. After ambitious attempts to find a suitable stretch of railway to run these two locomotives on, the only one which was practical and which became available at the right time was the three-mile Sheringham to Weybourne section of the former M&GNJR Melton Constable to Cromer Beach branch.

Work started on rebuilding the line in 1965 but the big turning point came on 4th June 1967 when two steam locomotives and the unique *Quad-art* set of articulated coaches were delivered. This was to me, and many others no doubt, the point when the more practical dreams of the Society looked to be within reach. It was then that my three parallel interests of photography, railways and the county of Norfolk were able to find a common focus, and I have enjoyed recording the development of the railway from then on.

The late 1960s were years of hope rather than solid achievement — new rolling stock and a loco arrived and tentative steamings of the J15 and the *Peckett* took place — but internal disagreements over aims held up development for a considerable time. 1969 saw the launch of the operating company, North Norfolk Railway Co. Ltd., and a share issue was promoted successfully with much national publicity. Amidst renewed interest, the long drawn-out procedure for obtaining the two Light Railway Orders that would allow the North Norfolk Railway to carry the public began. There were regulations to comply with, reams of paperwork to be completed, a firm organisation to be established and locos and other mechanical plant to be brought up to the required standards. After a successful Public Enquiry for the first LRO, the railway was able to run trains under licence from British Rail and then, after the granting of the second of the LROs, became an independent railway.

Since then the railway has established itself as part of the local community, with an increasing number of passengers every year. The enormous capital costs of further development and restoration dictate that progress is bound to be steady rather than spectacular. With the engineering side of the railway moving to the revitalised Weybourne station, with prospects for extension over Kelling Heath near to becoming a reality and with long-awaited progress on the B12, there is much to look forward to — and much more to photograph.

In the compilation of this selection of photographs I have avoided any positive attempt to show work being done. It would be impossible to show fairly all aspects of the enormous extent and variety of the work on site or the equally tremendous amount of effort that has been expended away from the railway in restoration, fund raising, publicity, etc. I have therefore tried to show the North Norfolk Railway in operation since 1967 and hope that it will portray something of the results of all those years of effort.

Brian Fisher
February 1981

Front cover: J15 564 nears Weybourne, March 1980.

North Norfolk Railway Stocklist

Mainline steam locomotives

Number and name	*Type*	*Built*	*Builder*	*Works number*	*Arrived*	*Notes*
564	J15 0-6-0	1912	GER, Stratford	Order B70	6/67	(1)
8572	B12/3 4-6-0	1928	Beyer Peacock	6488	6/67	(2)

Notes
(1) GER class Y14, no. 564, LNER 7564, 5462, BR 65462, owner — M&GNJRS, status — 0; (2) LNER 8572, 1572, BR 61572, built as B12, rebuilt to B12/3 1933, owner — M&GNJRS, status — R.

Industrial steam locomotives

Number and name	*Type*	*Built*	*Builder*	*Works number*	*Arrived*	*Notes*
Pony	0-4-0ST	1912	Hawthorne Leslie	2918	-/72	(3)
Fireless	0-6-0	1929	W. G. Bagnall	2370	3/80	(4)
45 *Colwyn*	0-6-0ST	1933	Kitson & Co.	5470	8/71	(5)
Wissington	0-6-0ST	1938	Hudswell Clarke	1700	2/78	(6)
5 *John D. Hammer*	0-6-0ST	1939	Peckett & Sons	1970	4/69	(7)
Ring Haw	0-6-0ST	1940	Hunslet Engine Co.	1982	2/71	(8)
13 *Harlaxton*	0-6-0T	1941	Andrew Barclay	2107	12/74	(9)
Birchenwood	0-6-0ST	1944	W. G. Bagnall	2680	1/76	(10)
12	0-6-0T	1955	RSH	7845	7/74	(11)

Notes
(3) ex-Blyth Harbour Commission, owner — I. Hurst, status — R; (4) ex-Distillers Ltd, owner — M&GNJRS, status — A; (5) ex-Stewart & Lloyds Minerals Ltd, owner — B.W.T. Amies, status — 0; (6) ex-British Sugar Corporation Ltd, Wissington, owner — M&GNJRS, status — A; (7) ex-National Coal Board, Ashington Colliery, owner — NNR Co. Ltd, status A; (8) ex-Nassington Barrowden Mining Co., owner — NNR Co. Ltd, status — W; (9) ex-Stewart & Lloyds Minerals Ltd, owners — B.W.T. Amies and P. Morris, status — R; (10) ex-Market Overton (High Dyke), owners — I. Hurst and G. A. Perry, status — R; (11) ex-CEGB, Hams Hall Power Station, owner — P. McOwan, status — A.

Diesels

Number and name	*Type*	*Built*	*Builder*	*Works number*	*Arrived*	*Notes*
Dr. Harry	0-4-0DM	1945	John Fowler & Co.	4100001	2/74	(12)
3	0-4-0DM	1953	John Fowler & Co.	4210080	6/77	(13)
10	0-4-0DH	1963	English Electric	8431	5/77	(14)
79960	DRB 4w	1958	Waggon und Maschinenbau	Lot 30482	6/67	(15)
79963	DRB 4w	1958	Waggon und Maschinenbau	Lot 30482	6/67	(16)

Notes
(12) 80hp, ex-Fisons Ltd (formerly West Norfolk Chemical and Manure Co.) King's Lynn, owner — M&GNJRS, status — E; (13) 150hp, ex-North Western Gas Board, owner — NNR Co. Ltd, status — 0; (14) 260hp, ex-National Coal Board, owner — P. Morris, status — 0; (15) 150hp diesel railbus, chassis built by Waggon und Maschinenbau, Donauworth, West Germany, bodywork built by Eastern Coachworks, Lowestoft, ex-BR, owner — NNR Co. Ltd, status — W; (16) as for (15), owner — NNR Co. Ltd, status — 0.

Passenger Vehicles

Number	*Type*	*Built*	*Builder*	*Order number*	*Arrived*	*Notes*
1	L&Y Saloon	1906	L&YR, Horwich	Diagram 80	4/69	(17)
295	GER BTK	1907	GER, Stratford	—	6/67	(18)
5318	LNWR Saloon	1913	LNWR, Wolverton	—	4/69	(19)
48941/2/3/4	Quad-art	1924	LNER, Doncaster	—	6/67	(20)
040923	LNER BZ	1929	LNER, Doncaster	—	3/71	(21)
3395	LNER TK	1930	Metro Cammell	—	12/79	(22)
87	Trailer	1932	Metro Cammell	—	3/75	(23)
91	Driver	1932	Metro Cammell	—	3/75	(24)
51769	LNER RB	1937	LNER, York	—	12/79	(25)
70621	LNER BG	1945	LNER, York	Lot 1123	12/78	(26)
624	SLSTP	1951	BR, Derby	Lot 1628	12/78	(27)
3868	TSO	1953	BR, York	Lot 30080	4/69	(28)
43034	CL	1954	BR, Doncaster	Lot 30094	3/75	(29)
43357	BS	1954	BR, York	Lot 30087	5/77	(30)
46147	S	1954	BR, Wolverton	Lot 30038	1/78	(31)
43041	CL	1955	BR, Doncaster	Lot 30094	3/75	(32)
43359	BS	1955	BR, York	Lot 30087	1/78	(33)
48026	SLO	1955	BR, Doncaster	Lot 30092	3/75	(34)
21103	BCK	1956	Metro Cammell	Lot 30185	12/78	(35)

Notes
(17) LMS 10701, 45037, BR M45037M, owner — M&GNJRS, status — A; (18) LNER 62377, BR Departmental DE 320325, *Norfolk Coast Express* stock, owners — M&GNJRS and Great Eastern Group, status — A; (19) LMS 10500, 45002, BR M45002M, owner — M&GNJRS, status — 0; (20) King's Cross Suburban Quad-art set 74, later LNER 86272/3/4/5, BR E86762/3/4/5E, owner — NNR Co. Ltd, status — A; (21) 4w passenger luggage van, BR E040923E, owner — P. McOwan, status — 0; (22) Gresley Third Corridor, later LNER 12493, BR E12493E, Departmental DE 320877, delivered to Norwich Victoria 9/76 for initial restoration, owner — M&GNJRS, status — R; (23) *Brighton Belle* Pullman parlour car no. 87, owner — Ind Coope, status — S; (24) *Brighton Belle* Pullman driving car no. 91, owner — Ind Coope, status — S; (25) Gresley buffet car, later LNER 9128, BR E9128E, delivered to Norwich Victoria 11/77 for initial restoration, owner — M&GNJRS, status — R; (26) Thompson bogie passenger luggage van, BR E70621E, owner — M&GNJRS, status — S; (27) Sleeping car, owner — NNR Co. Ltd, status — S; (28) Tourist Second Open, BR NE3868, in use as *Jubilee Coach* 1977, owner — NNR Co. Ltd, status — 0; (29) suburban Composite Lavatory, BR E43034, owner — M&GNJRS, status — 0; (30) suburban Brake Second, BR E43357, owner — NNR Co. Ltd, status — R; (31) suburban Second, BR E46147, arrived at Cambridge 1/78 for restoration, owner — M&GNJRS, status — R; (32) suburban Composite Lavatory, BR E43041, owner — M&GNJRS, status — 0; (33) suburban Brake Second, BR E43359, arrived at Cambridge 1/78 for restoration, owner — M&GNJRS, status — R; (34) suburban Second Lavatory Open, owner — M&GNJRS, status — 0; (35) Brake Composite Corridor, BR E21103, owner — NNR Co. Ltd, status — 0.

Goods Vehicles

Number	*Type*	*Built*	*Builder*	*Order number*	*Arrived*	*Notes*
—	Flat wagon	1890	Dallam Forge, Heywood	—	11/70	(36)
—	Flat wagon	1901	Harrison & Camm	—	-/70	(37)
4807	Van	1908		—	-/70	(38)
12	Steam crane	1919	Carrick & Wardale	—	6/77	(39)
—	Van	?	—	—	11/79	(40)
—	Van	?	—	—	11/79	(41)
—	Van	?	—	—	11/79	(42)
—	Van	?	—	—	11/79	(43)
—	Van	?	—	—	11/79	(44)
—	Van	?	—	—	11/79	(45)
—	Hopper	?	—	Diagram 12	11/79	(46)
—	Hopper	?	—	Diagram 12	11/79	(47)
421220	5-plank	1936	LMS	—	-/74	(48)
124148	5-plank	1936	GWR, Swindon	—	-/73	(49)
163058	Tanker	1942	Hurst Nelson	—	7/77	(50)
DS1749	Crane	1943	Booths, Ashford	—	6/73	(51)
164686	Tanker	1944	Hurst Nelson	—	-/70	(52)
55169	Brakevan	1944	SR, Ashford	—	-/73	(53)
756939	Vanfit	1949	BR, Wolverton	—	4/73	(54)
755094	Fruit van	1950	BR, Darlington	Lot 2134	-/74	(55)
904093	Lowmac	1950	BR, Swindon	Lot 2324	3/78	(56)
92097	Pasfruit	1953	BR, Swindon	—	3/75	(57)

Notes
(36) ex-Stewart & Lloyds Minerals Ltd, owner — M&GNJRS, status — 0; (37) ex-J. J. Colman Ltd, Norwich, converted from van, owner — M&GNJRS, status — 0; (38) ex-J. J. Colman Ltd, Norwich, mustard van, owner — M&GNJRS, status — A; (39) ex-W. & C. French Ltd, Wisbech, works number 12, owner — M&GNJRS, status — A; (40) ex-GER then British Sugar Corporation, Cantley, owner — M&GNJRS, status — K; (41) (42) (43) (44) (45) ex-GER then British Sugar Corporation, Cantley, owner — NNR Co. Ltd, status — K; (46) ex-British Sugar Corporation, Cantley, owner — M&GNJRS, status — A; (47) ex-British Sugar Corporation, Cantley, owner — NNR Co. Ltd, status — 0; (48) (49) 12 ton open wagon, owner — NNR Co. Ltd, status — 0; (50) 14 ton petrol tanker, ex-Esso Petroleum Ltd, owner — M&GNJRS, status — 0; (51) 12 ton lift manually operated crane, owner — P. Morris, status — 0; (52) 14 ton petrol tanker, ex-Shell Petroleum Ltd, owner — M&GNJRS, status — 0; (53) 25 ton goods brake van, owner — NNR Co. Ltd, status — 0; (54) (55) 12 ton van, owner — NNR Co. Ltd, status — 0; (56) 20 ton low loader, owner — M&GNJRS, status — 0; (57) 10 ton passenger fruit van, owner — M&GNJRS, status — 0.

Operational status—key

A—awaiting restoration; E—static exhibit; K—storage use; O—operational; R—being restored; S—static use; W—awaiting overhaul.

North Norfolk Railway Album

1. The arrival of the M&GN Joint Railway Society's J15 and B12 steam locomotives at Sheringham on 4th June 1967 was a landmark in the railway's history.

2. Whilst in storage at March MPD the locos had their cladding removed for boiler inspections and thus presented a rather sorry appearance when they stood in Sheringham sidings.

3. The J15 was put in steam occasionally in 1968 but was later found to have an unrepairable crack in the firebox which necessitated the rebuilding of the firebox in the 1970s.

4. Class B12/3 No. 61572, seen here on 19th January 1969, occasionally underwent preventive maintenance but otherwise was kept in store until it was restored externally in later years.

5. The LNWR Directors' Saloon and a BR TSO coach, together with the unseen L&Y Directors' Saloon, were slowly drawn past Sheringham East signal box on 26th April 1969.

6. After delivering the Directors' Saloons, Brush A1A-A1A D5569 — the last BR loco to pass through Sheringham station — runs to collect its brake van before departing.

7. Later the same day, Peckett No. 5 hauls the newly-delivered coaches along the singled track into Sheringham station's platform 1 for the benefit of a BBC film crew.

8. An early train for members hauled by Hunslet 0-6-0ST *Ring Haw* passes Golf Links Crossing at Easter 1971. The siding to the buffer stop on the left was lifted soon afterwards.

9. In the spring of 1972, RSH 0-6-0T No. 40 shunts a third-class brake built by the GER in 1907 for the *Norfolk Coast Express.* No. 40 is now on the Colne Valley Railway.

10. 0-6-0 tanks *Colwyn* and Peckett No. 5 were turned to face *up-the-hill* to give better steaming. Sheringham East signal box was moved to near its present site on the same day, 8th July 1972.

11. *Colwyn* shunts a variety of industrial tanks — 0-4-0ST *Pony,* 0-6-0T *Harlaxton* and 0-6-0T No. 12 on 15th March 1975. *Pony* and *Harlaxton* have since undergone heavy overhauls.

12. For two days in May 1973 the railway was the scene of filming of a Dad's Army episode *The Royal Train*, with *Colwyn* and the GER coach starring at Weybourne.

13. The chase sequence, filmed from a flat wagon at the rear of the train, featured the pump trolley manned by some of the regular characters from the TV series.

14. For several years the *Peckett* and the Gresley *Quad-art* set of articulated coaches seen here on 10th April 1974, were a regular and unique combination, handling most trains.

15. *Peckett* and *Quads* again, being filmed for Sir John Betjeman's film *A Passion for Churches.* Sir John Betjeman is a Joint President of the M&GN Joint Railway Society.

16. 80hp diesel *Dr. Harry,* formerly the Muck Works shunter at King's Lynn, was rescued from a scrap merchant in 1973 and performed gallantly in the rebuilding of the railway.

17. The rail connection to BR having been removed in road improvements, temporary track was laid on the night of 15/16th March 1975 to take delivery of *Brighton Belle* and suburban coaches.

18. After the coaches had been propelled across Station Road, *Operation Coachbelle,* as the 18 hour operation was known, was put into reverse to restore the road to public use.

19. A typical view of an operating steam railway — a neatly caught tablet as Hunslet 0-6-0ST *Ring Haw* pulls in Norwich by a group of enthusiasts before delivery to Sheringham by road from Cromer. Enthusiasts pro

ingham station in April 1980. The first coach, a brake composite corridor of 1956, was renovated and repainted
ally the entire workforce — both for restoring trains and for running them!

20. The J15 firebox was rebuilt by contractors and lifted onto the frames on 20th January 1977. The *Peckett* shunted the J15 to platform 1 for restoration to continue.

21. Several other crane lifts were carried out on the same day; here *Harlaxton's* boiler and firebox were prepared to go to contractors for specialist attention.

22. Work on the J15 restoration continued apace and by 12th March 1977 progress was evident, even though working conditions were not always of the best.

23. Restoration has to go on alongside the operation of the railway; here the *Peckett,* by then named *John D. Hammer,* prepares to return to Sheringham on 3rd April 1977.

24. In Jubilee Year 1977, the TSO coach was repainted in appropriate colours and formed part of many trains like this one passing Sheringham Golf Course on 21st July 1977.

25. The J15 underwent several steam tests and trial runs during the summer of 1977. On 9th August the English Electric diesel-hydraulic loco performs station pilot duties.

26. Kitson 0-6-0ST *Colwyn* makes a spirited attack on an up gradient with a lengthy train of two suburban coaches and the *Quad-art* set on 28th May 1978.

27. B12/3 4-6-0 61572 was restored externally to BR black livery for display at Sheringham but is seen here on 16th October 1977 at Weybourne awaiting the J15 Recommissioning Celebrations.

28. The two diesel railbuses have proved popular with the public due to the excellent views obtained from them. They are also popular with school parties on non-steaming days.

29. A week before the J15 Recommissioning Ceremony, former Norwich Thorpe shedmaster Bill Harvey oversees the finishing touches to the loco, one of his old allocation.

30. Recommissioning Day, 22nd October 1977, and the sparkling J15 runs round at Weybourne in preparation for taking the crowded special train back to Sheringham.

31. A special freight train was run later on the Recommissioning Day purely for pleasure and photography. It is seen here on the 1 in 80 climb into Weybourne station.

32. Again on 22nd October 1977 and at the country end of the line. The J15 is the subject of much photography as it runs round at Weybourne under Bridge 302.

33. No. 564, in its attractive but temporary GER First World War austerity grey livery, accelerates vigorously away from Golf Links Crossing on 7th April 1980. Note the GER headcode!

34. Sheringham station from the shunter's viewpoint with *Brighton Belle* motorcoach in Platform 1, *Colwyn*, J15 and other locos in Platform 2 and a railbus in the *fourth road.*

35. The railway takes an active part in Sheringham Carnival Week, and the 1978 Miss Sheringham, Karin Farncombe, poses on the smartly repainted ex-BSC 0-6-0ST loco *Wissington.*

36. Hunslet 0-6-0ST *Ring Haw,* a mainstay of the loco department in the 1979 and 1980 seasons, takes a Sheringham to Weybourne train over Bridge 303 on 15th July 1979.

37. Another special freight was run after the M&GN Society's AGM on 17th May 1980. 0T1, an Eastern Counties open-top bus, provided photographers with a good mobile vantage point!

38. A Sheringham station scene, even with a typical sea-mist in the background, with passengers leaving a recent arrival and the J15 being made ready to take out the next train.

39. The special freight train on 17th May 1980 again, this time crossing the coast road at Bridge 303 on the way to Weybourne. The standard of restoration is noteworthy.

40. *Colwyn* and *Ring Haw* run round at the end of the line on 8th September 1979. Negotiations were then well under way for purchase of the old track bed over Kelling Heath.

41. A characteristic five-coach train of the 1980 summer season on the embankment alongside Sheringham golf course, tackling the start of the 1 in 97 gradient.

42. Ex-NCB English Electric diesel hydraulic loco 10 carries out the very useful function of station pilot in the carriage sidings at Sheringham on 12th August 1980.

43. In July 1980 *Ring Haw* and the J15 with the *Quads,* sporting added mock clerestories, were used in the filming of the BBC serialisation of D. H. Lawrence's *Sons and Lovers.*

44. The J15, repainted in green as GNR No. 564 on 1st July 1980, pulls into Weybourne which, in turn, was standing in as seaside resort Mablethorpe in *Sons and Lovers.*

45. The summer of 1980 saw greatly accelerated progress on the engine shed at Weybourne where rebuilding work went on while the regular train services continued as usual.

46. On 1st February 1981 in the newly-occupied engine shed were re-liveried 0-4-0DH No. 10 with Bagnall 0-6-0ST *Birchenwood* in the foreground. Just visible behind the Bagnall is *Ring Haw.*